CW01263977

Viking Nottinghamshire

Rebecca Gregory
Introduction by Judith Jesch

For John and June

Viking Nottinghamshire

Rebecca Gregory
Introduction by Judith Jesch

Five Leaves Publications
www.fiveleaves.co.uk

Viking Nottinghamshire
Rebecca Gregory
Introduction by Judith Jesch

Copyright © Rebecca Gregory 2017
Introduction © Judith Jesch

Published in 2017 by
Five Leaves Publications,
14a Long Row, Nottingham NG1 2DH
www.fiveleaves.co.uk
www.fiveleavesbookshop.co.uk

ISBN: 978-1-910170-47-2

Printed in Great Britain

Contents

Introduction

Drivers entering Nottinghamshire are met by signs welcoming them to 'Robin Hood County'. A statue of Robin Hood is a prominent landmark in the City of Nottingham. To both residents and visitors, this legendary, and largely fictional, figure has come to represent the medieval history of both the county and the city. Yet if we go beyond the green-clad archer, Nottingham's importance in an earlier period becomes clear, when it was one of the Five Boroughs of the Danelaw, and when Nottinghamshire was widely settled by Scandinavian immigrants known as Vikings. This book brings that hidden history into view.

There are several reasons why the Viking Age (and earlier Anglo-Saxon) past of Nottinghamshire is not obvious to the casual observer. There has been relatively little archaeological activity on sites from this period. Where there have been major digs, such as in the City of Nottingham in the 1970s, these are not widely known and still not published. This makes it hard even for academic specialists to understand what was going on and to communicate their results to the general public. Above ground, there is important stone sculpture from the period, still in medieval parish churches around the county, but these monuments are also very little known or understood. That will change now that the Nottinghamshire volume of the *Corpus of Anglo-Saxon Stone Sculpture* has been published in 2016. Other than these material traces, there are few contemporary documents which mention Nottingham or its shire in a meaningful way. Important and extensive evidence for the early medieval period can, however, be found in place-names. These names of towns, villages and streets are key to understanding what happened in Nottinghamshire and the East Midlands in the Viking Age and are given their full due in this book.

This is the first book dedicated to Nottinghamshire in the Viking Age. The idea of highlighting the county's Viking heritage goes back to 1985 when Professor Christine Fell OBE persuaded the University of Nottingham to set up a Lectureship in Viking Studies – I was the lucky person who got the job. Some years later, Ross Bradshaw suggested to me that a book on Viking

Nottinghamshire would be a useful addition to his list at Five Leaves. It took a while, but the best things are worth waiting for. The knowledge we have gained in this time from developments in archaeology, including the Portable Antiquities Scheme, the publication of the Corpus volume noted above, and the extensive work of the Institute for Name-Studies at the University of Nottingham, means that this book is much better now than if it had been written even ten years ago. We are also very lucky to have had Dr Rebecca Gregory, an expert on the place-names of Nottinghamshire, but also thoroughly trained in all aspects of Viking and Anglo-Saxon studies at the University of Nottingham, to write it. Without funding from the University's British Identities Research Priority Area the writing of this book would not have been possible.

Welcome to Viking Nottinghamshire!

Judith Jesch
Professor of Viking Studies, University of Nottingham

1. How the story starts

The story of Viking Nottinghamshire is one which encompasses much more than the conflict and violence which are often seen to be among the defining characteristics of the **Viking Age**. The influence of Scandinavian conquerors and settlers on the county of Nottinghamshire is about more, and more complex, things than military might and political dominance, and can be seen in many different forms in the county as we know it today. Some of these forms are easy to spot, hiding in plain sight as we go about our daily lives; others are more subtle and easily overlooked.

The Viking Age in England ended when William the Conqueror, the first **Norman** king of England, invaded the country in 1066. Viking Nottinghamshire, however, did not simply disappear with the advent of Norman rule, but is present to this day, underlying the county's administration, its settlement patterns and place-names, its regional identity and culture, and has undoubtedly had a profound effect on the development of not just the city of Nottingham, but other urban areas such as Newark and Mansfield, and also the rural countryside which forms a large part of the present-day county. This book will tell that story, from the events that brought the Viking settlers to Nottingham-shire to the archaeological, linguistic and documentary clues which tell us how and where their lasting legacy made its mark.

Some technical terms are used throughout this book: these are given in bold the first time they are used in each chapter, and can be found in the glossary at the back of the book. Also included is a timeline of key events for Viking Nottinghamshire, along with some suggestions for further reading, places to visit and things to look out for in the county.

Nottinghamshire before the Vikings

The Viking Age in England is generally agreed to have begun in the late eighth century, when we have a written account of a raid by

ANGLO-SAXON KINGDOMS c. 800 AD

Picts

Northumbria

Offa's Dyke

Welsh

Mercia

East Anglia

Essex

Sussex

Wessex

Kent

Welsh

© the author and Graeme Thornhill, 2017

Figure 1: Map of the Anglo-Saxon kingdoms in England

Scandinavian pirates on the monastery of St Cuthbert, which was situated on Lindisfarne, a small tidal island off the north-east coast of England, about ten miles south-east of Berwick-upon-Tweed. This is almost certainly not the first such raid, but it is the first that is recorded with a reliable date, and it marked the beginning of a pattern of small raids on churches round the English coast over the following decades. This is how the Vikings first became known to the **Anglo-Saxons**: as seafaring raiders. The **Old Norse** word *víkingr* indicates someone who undertook exactly this kind of activity, and the **Old English** word *wīcing*, first recorded following a significant battle between Viking and Anglo-Saxon forces at Maldon in Essex in 991, also meant something like 'pirate', and seems to have been used by the English to indicate seafaring Scandinavians in particular. There is no evidence, though, that the Vikings used the word to refer to themselves in an English context.

At that time, Nottinghamshire as we know it did not exist. Counties were not yet used as administrative units, and the geographical area which was to become the modern county did not have its own particular identity. England was not even a unified country in the eighth century. Anglo-Saxon England was divided into kingdoms which had been founded and developed after the Anglo-Saxons arrived from mainland Europe, with each of the kingdoms having its own rulers and political stances (fig. 1). Nottingham fell within the kingdom of **Mercia**, and is only eighteen miles from Repton, an important religious and royal centre in the kingdom. Mercia was one of the three largest kingdoms in England, along with Northumbria and Wessex, although there were other smaller kingdoms which continued to be ruled separately. Mercia had been firmly Christian since the seventh century, and churches were part of the landscape, although few Anglo-Saxon churches survive today as the vast majority of them were built in wood, not stone.

Nottingham would have been an important Anglo-Saxon settlement, in an ideal location for travel, trade and defence alongside the River Trent. Its name comes from the Old English language spoken by the Anglo-Saxons, and means 'homestead of Snot's people'. Snot was an Anglo-Saxon man's name, and the place-name indicates somewhere where he and his followers – perhaps his family, or his tribe – settled down. One of the earliest records we have of the place-name is from

1086, maybe 500 years after the Anglo-Saxon settlement was founded, when it was spelt *Snotingaham* (fig. 2). Sneinton, now part of the conurbation of Nottingham, also takes its name from Snot, this time with the Old English word for a farm or village: *tūn*.

The countryside further outside Nottingham was also settled by the Anglo-Saxons, with a range of small villages and farmsteads supporting various-sized groups of people. Roman roads would still have been used by travellers and traders, as would the Trent and its smaller tributaries flowing through the county. The Trent was wider and shallower than the modern river as it passed through medieval Nottinghamshire, in some places consisting of several smaller channels of water rather than one large one, and would have been fordable on foot or horseback in some places. These locations are often usefully marked by place-names such as Wilford 'willow-tree ford' and Shelford 'shallow ford', both named in Old English. By the eighth century, Anglo-Saxon settlements could be found across the county, especially concentrated in well-connected areas with access to good-quality land for farming. The Anglo-Saxons practised mixed farming, with some land ploughed for crops, some used as meadow or pasture for grazing animals, and

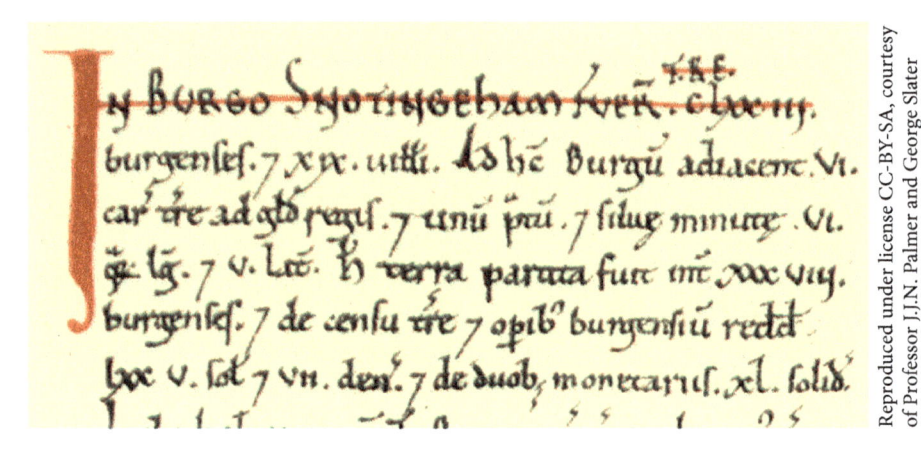

Figure 2: Excerpt from Domesday Book showing the entry for Nottingham, taken from Open Domesday at opendomesday.org/place/SK5739.nottingham/

woodland used for timber and additional pasture. Heavily-wooded areas were less popular for settlement, although the Anglo-Saxons certainly cleared trees in many places to make more room for farming, and built settlements in previously-wooded locations.

The area that would become Nottinghamshire was thoroughly settled in Anglo-Saxon times, and the aspects that made the county so appealing for Anglo-Saxon settlers – its varied landscape, its rivers and fertile farmland, its central position and accessibility by land and water – made it just as desirable a place to settle for other groups from across the North Sea.

2. Incursions

The beginnings

To return to the island of Lindisfarne, off the coast of what was then the kingdom of Northumbria, we have the raid which is seen to mark the beginning of the Viking incursions in Britain. Much of what we know about this event, and indeed about much of this period of history, is taken from a document (or, more accurately, a set of closely-related documents) known as the **Anglo-Saxon Chronicle**. The Chronicle recorded the significant happenings each year, although we are at the mercy of the chroniclers as to which events they perceived to be significant, and therefore worthy of inclusion. The Chronicle was originally one document, created in the late ninth century, and this document was copied multiple times and distributed to monasteries across the country where each version was updated according to that monastery's own priorities. The Chronicle survives in nine manuscripts in various states of completeness, and we therefore have several versions of some events, in more or less detail as the compiler saw fit in each case. However, the Chronicle records predominantly the same kinds of information in each of its iterations. Many of the aspects of history which interest modern researchers are not the deaths of kings and bishops, which the Chronicle frequently recounts, but the day-to-day life of medieval people, which isn't so well-recorded in documents.

The Anglo-Saxon Chronicle is still an important source despite its narrow focus. In the entry for the year 793 which records the raid on Lindisfarne, the Chronicle tells us:

> ...on the sixth day before the ides of January, the woeful inroads of heathen men destroyed God's church in Lindisfarne island by fierce robbery and slaughter.

The word 'heathen' is important in this entry: it refers to the fact that the Vikings were not Christian at this time, in contrast to the Anglo-Saxons, who had been converted (at least officially) in the seventh century. The Viking raiders, therefore, would not have regarded the monastery at Lindisfarne to be sacred in their own religion, although they certainly would have recognised it as a special and significant place for its inhabitants and for other communities in Anglo-Saxon England. The monastery of St Cuthbert would have been targeted not because of its religious status, but simply because churches and monasteries were among the wealthiest institutions within reach of the North Sea, and they tended to be isolated, making them prime targets for piracy.

From this date onwards, small hit-and-run raids on the coast of England continued, and loot from English churches has been found in **Viking Age** graves in Scandinavia: we don't know exactly what brought the Vikings to England, but we do know where some of the treasure ended up. At this time the area that would become Nottinghamshire was unaffected by Viking activity, as it was far enough inland to be immune to the type of raiding taking place in coastal areas. But the nature of the Vikings' relationship with England was soon to change.

Conquest

The Anglo-Saxon Chronicle is also our best source for what happened next. In 865 the military force known as the Great Heathen Army began its progress across England. This army was made up of many groups of warriors from Scandinavia and elsewhere, banded together under shared leadership. This was a different group of people from the piratical raiders who had attacked the coast, and their motivations were different too; this time the Vikings meant to acquire land for themselves and take a permanent place in England.

Beginning in East Anglia, the army worked their way northwards to York, which they conquered in 867 (fig. 3). In 868, the Chronicle tells

865-67 ———
870-73 ———
874 ———

York

Torksey

Repton Nottingham

Cambridge

THE GREAT
HEATHEN ARMY

Figure 3: Map showing key parts of the journeys made by the Great Heathen Army in the late ninth century

us, 'the same army went into Mercia to Nottingham, and there fixed their winter-quarters.' Although the Mercians assembled a military force to confront the Vikings, 'there was no heavy fight; for the Mercians made peace with the army.' In fact, the combined forces of the Mercian and West Saxon kings laid siege to Nottingham but could not recapture it, so they agreed to let the Viking army leave Nottingham and return to York. It is difficult to know what effect this short stay in Nottingham might have had, but even if there is no direct evidence of any physical impact on the town or its surroundings, the psychological effect on the local population would certainly have been significant.

The Great Heathen Army continued its travels, settling at Torksey in Lindsey (now in Lincolnshire) in 873, where the Mercians again 'made peace' rather than battle with the Vikings. The following year they travelled to Repton (in Derbyshire), and the Chronicle tells us that they 'subdued all that land', meaning the kingdom of Mercia. This time, there were lasting consequences.

Who were the Great Heathen Army?

The places where the Great Heathen Army spent the winter months, waiting for more favourable weather to continue its campaign, are important for a number of reasons. The extended length of time that a large group spent in one location would be expected to leave a much greater trace in the archaeological record than that same group on the move, partly through cemeteries associated with the camps, partly through chance loss of small items over a limited area, and partly through activities which can leave a long-lasting trace, such as some kinds of crafting and metalworking.

While the Anglo-Saxon Chronicle tells us a good deal about the army's movements, it gives us very little in the way of description of the people themselves, and this means that historians have been debating questions such as the size of the army for many years. Estimates have varied from the hundreds to the thousands, and the type of people who travelled with the army has been questioned just as much. Was it only fighting men – a purely military force – or did the warriors bring their families with them, hoping to find a new home once the fighting was done?

Archaeologists have begun to find answers to these questions by looking at the sites of the winter camps. The camp at Nottingham cannot

Figure 4: A selection of the lead gaming pieces found at the site of the Great Heathen Army's camp at Torksey, Lincolnshire, used in the winter of 873/4. 289 gaming pieces in total were found by metal detector at Torksey up to August 2015. The hollow shape of the gaming pieces would have meant that some could be stacked together

be located, mainly because the city is now so large that buildings cover any potential archaeological site. However, the situation at Torksey, about thirty miles north-east of Nottingham, is very different. The army over-wintered there in 873, and the site has not become urbanised as Nottingham has, meaning that archaeologists have been able to investigate it thoroughly in recent years.

They found evidence for trade and exchange, including coins and **bullion** used as currency, along with weights to determine the value of the bullion. There may even have been coins minted during the Great Heathen Army's campaign. As well as buying and selling, people worked metal, wood and textiles inside the camp, and the archaeologists discovered hundreds of lead gaming pieces (fig. 4), suggesting that the army must have had some leisure time over the long winter nights.

The site of the camp was found to be about fifty-five hectares (a hectare is roughly the same size as an international rugby pitch, so you could think about fifty-five of those, or forty-four cricket pitches, seventy-six football pitches, or four Meadowhalls). A camp this size would be large enough to accommodate an army numbering in the thousands – probably between 1,500 and 5,000 soldiers – with a large number of traders and craftworkers, and perhaps even women and children, able to travel alongside them.

There is substantial evidence to suggest that women were part of the group travelling as the Great Heathen Army. The finds at Torksey relating to textiles might reflect the presence of women, as textile working was generally undertaken by women rather than men. The presence of women as part of the group is further supported by excavations undertaken at Repton in the 1970s: archaeologists investigated a burial mound and several cemeteries at the site of the winter camp there, and found that women's bodies made up 18% of the dead in the main burial mound, and as many as 37% in the associated cemeteries. The Anglo-Saxon Chronicle entries for the years 893 and 895 describe women and children from the Great Heathen Army being taken as hostages by the English. Although these accounts are from a later date than the winter camps at Repton and Torksey, and from elsewhere in the country, there is no reason to suggest that the makeup of the group should differ significantly between those dates and locations. Two fragments of Scandinavian-style brooches were also found at Torksey, although unconnected to the main excavations. Fragments are more problematic as evidence for women's presence than whole brooches would be, as they may not have actually been wearable brooches at the time they were lost or thrown away, but it is possible that whole brooches could have been damaged by ploughing or other means after being deposited in the ground. While they aren't solid evidence of women being part of the army and its entourage, they add further to the picture built up by documentary, burial, and craftworking evidence.

This, then, seems to have been the group of Vikings described as the Great Heathen Army: thousands of soldiers from different parts of Scandinavia and further afield, and an entourage of families and craftspeople looking to make their new home in England. Although Torksey is the only winter camp about which we have this much information so far, excavations are currently underway at Repton (fig. 5), where the army over-wintered the following year. Archaeologists are

© Cat Jarman, 2017, reproduced by kind permission

Figure 5: A team of archaeologists working at Repton in the summer of 2017. These excavations are just outside a small ditched area previously thought to be the extent of the Viking winter camp.

looking for evidence of the size of the camp and the kinds of activities which took place within it, in order to learn more about the Great Heathen Army as it progressed.

3. Settlement

After the **Great Heathen Army** had 'subdued' **Mercia**, the Vikings were in a position to be able to start making themselves at home in their newly-conquered land. From Repton, the army separated, and while one group went north, the remaining force went to Cambridge 'and settled there for a year', leaving a man called Ceowulf, an **Anglo-Saxon** nobleman who had sworn allegiance to the Vikings, in charge of Mercia while they were away. The army travelled from Cambridge to Wareham in Dorset, then to Exeter, and in 877 they 'went into the land of Mercia and shared out some of it'. Much of what we know about the decades which followed this first Viking settlement in Nottinghamshire has to be pieced together from small snippets of evidence.

Information on the population of medieval England is scarce, especially for the period before the Norman Conquest. For the most part, 'normal' people don't appear in documentary sources, and there was no such thing as a medieval English census. The closest thing we have to an estimate of early medieval population is the **Domesday Book**, a survey made in 1086 by order of William the Conqueror, the first **Norman** king of England. The survey was made primarily to assess taxation, so it is more concerned with land values than with population, but from the people recorded in the Domesday Book we can make a rough estimate of Nottinghamshire's population in the late eleventh century. Historians believe that Nottinghamshire probably held something between 25,000 and 30,000 people: this is similar to the population of Sutton-in-Ashfield in 2011. The Domesday Book records no information at all about the general population, so it can't help us to determine how many might have been Scandinavian immigrants in the previous centuries – we have to assess other kinds of evidence to discover their presence.

The names of towns and villages can be crucial in detecting where different groups of people settled, based in part on the languages those people spoke. To understand place-name evidence, we have to understand how place-names were created and developed. They originally worked as descriptive labels: they weren't 'bestowed' for effect as some names are now. Settlers would name a place according to something unique about it; this might be the people living there, the kind of farming or industry for which it was known, a useful resource found nearby, or proximity to a distinctive landscape feature. Because they were used as labels, we know that place-names were originally given in a language the local people could understand: otherwise, the label would be of no practical use. The Viking settlers spoke **Old Norse**, whereas the Anglo-Saxons spoke **Old English**. Anglo-Saxon place-names, therefore, were given in Old English, while new names for Viking settlements would have been given in the settlers' language, Old Norse. The presence of Old Norse words in place-names means that local people would have been able to speak enough Old Norse to understand that place-name, and therefore may have been Viking settlers, or Anglo-Saxons in close contact with them.

The pattern of Old Norse place-names in Nottinghamshire shows that Vikings settled across the county (fig. 6). The most common Old Norse words in place-names are *bý*, meaning 'farm or village', and *thorp*, meaning 'secondary settlement', somewhere less important or self-sufficient than a *bý*. Take a look at the road signs while you travel around Nottinghamshire and you're quite likely to see at least one place-name ending in *-thorp* or *-by*, which gives away its Viking origins.

It is difficult to know how much conflict would have been involved in this first stage of Viking settlement in the county. There was certainly enough available land for communities of Scandinavians to have their own farms and villages without encroaching on Anglo-Saxon settlements, and the pattern of Old Norse place-names shows a tendency for Viking settlements to be on less desirable land, suggesting that – in some cases, at least – they simply settled for the land the Anglo-Saxons didn't want. If this was the case, it is possible that settlement was a fairly peaceful process, at least for the ordinary people.

Figure 6: This map shows the parish names in Nottinghamshire which are entirely made up of Old Norse words. They are likely to indicate some of the first places in the county where groups of Viking settlers made their homes.

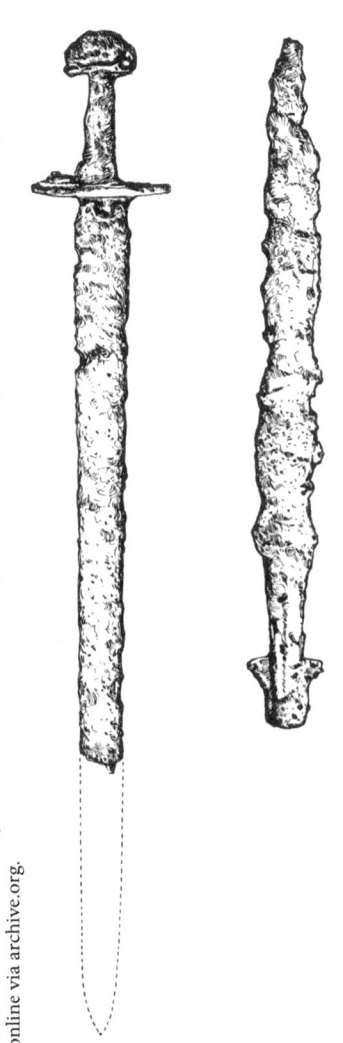

Figure 7: Line drawings of an iron sword and spearhead found in or near Nottingham in 1851, now held by Royal Armouries, catalogue number XI.7957 and VII.3049. The sword is classified as a Peterson type X, meaning that it has a pommel but no guard, and dates from the tenth or eleventh century. This type of sword is relatively common across central and northern Europe.

There is a small amount of archaeological evidence linked to weapons and warfare in Nottingham-shire, although not taken from the context of a battle site. An iron sword and a spearhead (fig. 7) were discovered in or close to Nottingham itself in 1851. Unfortunately, information about where and how they were found is confused, but contemporary illustrations of them were made, and there are several accounts which suggest that they were probably found alongside at least one burial, presumably of a Viking man. Viking burials, especially in the early stages of settlement in England before conversion to Christianity, would contain items of significance (referred to by archaeologists as **grave goods**), buried alongside the body of the deceased. Grave goods can represent a literal role or occupation of the deceased person in life, or can have more complex relationships either to social standing and a role in the community, or to ideas about the afterlife. So placing a weapon or weapons in a man's grave could represent his role as a warrior, especially in this context of Viking conquest, but could also have wider symbolic significance. He might

have been a man of importance in the local community, and therefore be seen as deserving of a valuable item such as a sword being interred with him, or a weapon might be included in his burial to allow him to defend himself in the afterlife, whether or not he had needed to do so while he was alive. It is thought that weapons functioned, at least in a burial context, as badges of masculinity in the Viking Age, so it would be simplistic to assume that the presence of a sword or spear in a grave indicates the presence of a warrior. Another sword (fig. 8) was found in 1892 at Farndon, near Newark, while digging for improvements made to the local church. Like the Nottingham weapons, this location also suggests a **heathen** burial in the first stages of settlement in Nottinghamshire, with the sword again acting as part of the grave goods. This time the accounts of the discovery are much clearer, and we can be more confident that this was indeed a burial weapon based on the location and context of the find.

Other than these weapons, we have very few archaeological finds of strictly Viking origin in Nottinghamshire. One exception is a beautiful gold finger ring, found near Newark and recorded on the Portable Antiquities Scheme database (fig. 9). The Portable Antiquities Scheme is a means of recording small archaeological finds in England and Wales,

Figure 8: Iron sword found in a Viking Age burial at Farndon Church. This is a Peterson type V, which means that it has a trilobate (three-part) pommel and straight guards. It is dated to the earlier part of the tenth century. This type of sword is found widely across Europe, but has a higher concentration in Norway. The hilt on this type of sword is often decorated with silver or bronze. The sword is held in the British Museum, catalogue number 1906,0612.1.

especially those discovered by members of the public, and making information about those finds available online. Finger rings like this one could be worn by either men or women, and we have no way of knowing who the owner of this ring might have been, although the ring's value probably indicates a high-status owner. It is not clear whether the ring was lost, or intentionally buried.

The Danelaw

However peaceful rural settlement might have been, there was still conflict between the ruling powers of the Vikings and the Anglo-Saxons. In 878 King Alfred 'the Great' of Wessex won a decisive victory over Guthrum, one of the Great Heathen Army's leaders. Soon afterwards, a treaty was agreed between the two leaders. As part of this treaty, Guthrum agreed to convert to Christianity, and Alfred gave much of eastern England over to Danish control. This area was later to be known as the **Danelaw**, although this term was not used in the treaty. The boundary of the

Figure 9: Gold finger ring found near Newark. The ends were originally twisted together, but have been distorted while in the ground, and they are now almost untwisted. The form and decoration on the ring are typically Viking, dating from the late ninth to the tenth century. Information available on the Portable Antiquities Scheme database, object number DENO-9A6C17.

THE DANELAW
LATE 9TH CENTURY

York

Lincoln

Nottingham

Derby

Leicester   Stamford

Northampton

London

© the author and Graeme Thornhill, 2017

Figure 10: Map of the Danelaw, the area given over to Danish control in the ninth century. The map also shows the locations of the Five Boroughs, as well as London and York.

Danelaw stretched from London to the Mersey, and the area subject to Danish rule roughly comprised the modern counties of Bedfordshire, Buckinghamshire, Cambridgeshire, Derbyshire, Essex, Hertfordshire, Huntingdonshire, Leicestershire, Lincolnshire, Middlesex, Norfolk, Northamptonshire, Nottinghamshire, Suffolk, and Yorkshire (fig. 10).

Nottinghamshire was, therefore, firmly under Danish control in the late ninth century. This situation did not last for long, and the decades which followed Alfred and Guthrum's treaty were quite complicated. The part of the Great Heathen Army which had gone north from Repton in 875 eventually settled in part of the Kingdom of Northumbria, of which York was the seat of power. They had close links with the Kingdom of Dublin, and developed a different political and social identity from the Danish settlers based in the Kingdom of East Anglia. The settlers in the East Midlands were predominantly Danish too, but the influence of the Kingdom of York was also felt in various ways in nearby Nottinghamshire, including land held by the Archbishop of York in Southwell and elsewhere. Boundaries were not clear-cut in this period, and neither was regional identity.

The Anglo-Saxon Kingdom of Wessex began a campaign to regain control of the Danelaw in the early tenth century, and in 918 Nottingham was captured by King Edward the Elder. Rather than trying to expel the town's Danish occupants, however, Edward created a garrison in Nottingham manned by both English and Danish men. Nottingham already had one **burh** (fortification), but Edward built a second, on the opposite bank of the Trent, and also constructed a bridge between them. He ensured that whoever controlled Nottingham also controlled the river. Edward co-opted both the English and Danish occupants of Mercia against the Vikings of York, suggesting that by this point Danish or English origins were perhaps not as important as a shared interest in protecting the town of Nottingham.

By 924 Edward's son Edmund had captured Mercia from the 'Norsemen' of York, and Nottingham remained under English control. We might expect that this would be the end of the Danelaw, but this is not the case. We know that the Danelaw, although part of England, continued to be seen in many respects as a distinct entity at the end of the tenth century. In 997, King Aethelred II 'The Unready' issued two law codes which are usually seen as a pair, one of which applied to areas

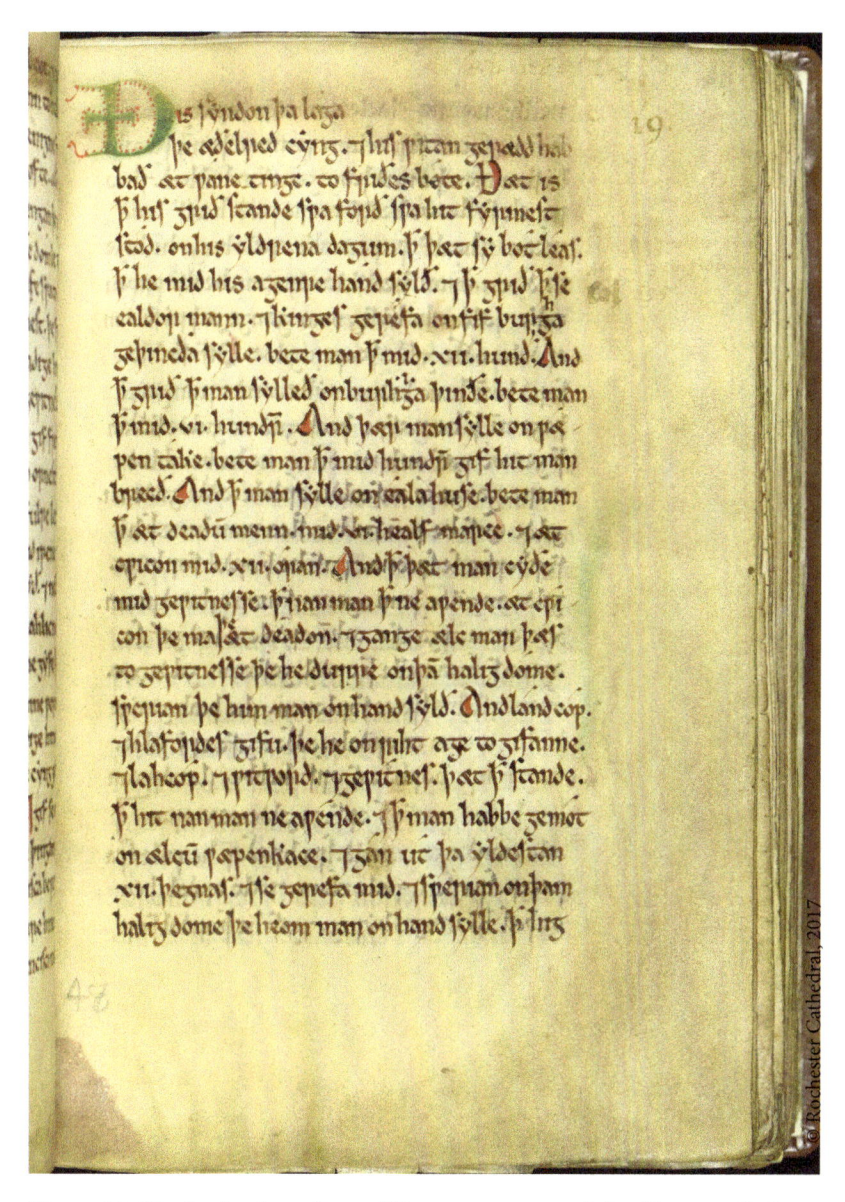

Figure 11: The beginning of a twelfth-century copy of the Wantage Code, taken from the *Textus Roffensis* at Rochester Cathedral. The *Textus Roffensis* and its companion, the *Custumale Roffensis*, are available to view online.

under English law, and the other to the Danelaw. The Danelaw code is known as the Wantage Code, named after the town of Wantage in Berkshire where it was issued. The Wantage Code now survives in a number of copies, one of which is held by Rochester Cathedral in the *Textus Roffensis* (fig. 11). The *Textus* is a twelfth-century compilation of a number of documents including early law codes, and is written in Old English and Latin.

Not only does this document show that the Danelaw was treated differently from the rest of England, but it also uses some other terms which relate specifically to Danelaw administration. It mentions the **Five Boroughs** (*fif burȝha*) (fig. 12), a confederation which consisted of the *burh*s of Nottingham, Derby, Leicester, Stamford and Lincoln. Four of these towns would later become county towns, and this is the first administrative entity which begins to look very much like the modern East Midlands. There is also a smaller unit mentioned in the text, the **wapentake** (*wapentace*) (fig. 13). A wapentake was made up of multiple parishes, and was smaller than a county. Elsewhere in England these units were called hundreds, but in the Danelaw a loanword from Old Norse, *vápnatak*, was used instead. This is a compound word from the Old Norse *vápn* 'weapon' and *taka* 'to take'. What the word refers to is uncertain, as the word *taka* could refer either to the brandishing of weapons (perhaps as a form of voting in an assembly), or could indicate the taking away of weapons, in preparation for an entirely unarmed meeting. The word was not used

Figure 12

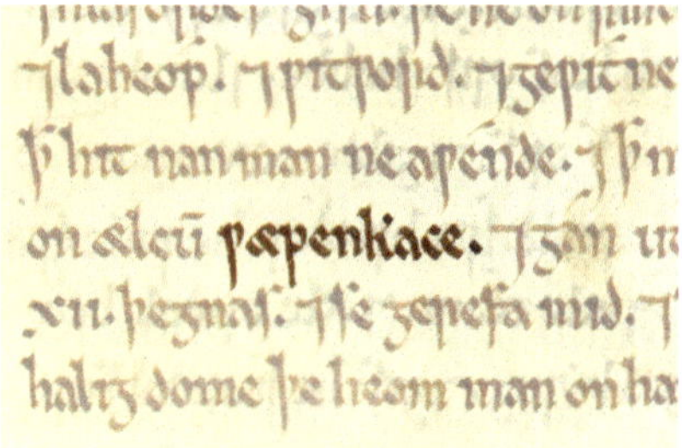

Figure 13

in Scandinavia to refer to administrative divisions, so it may have been applied in the Danelaw in a figurative rather than a literal sense, adopted as a rough equivalent to the English hundred. Whatever its meaning, however, the choice to replace the Old English term with an Old Norse one shows the extent of Viking control and influence in Nottinghamshire.

Local law and order

The hundred, or wapentake, was an important concept in medieval England. Before counties were recognised as administrative units, groups of parishes were organised in hundreds (wapentakes in the Danelaw), and within them courts and assemblies were held where justice was enacted by and on behalf of the people of that wapentake, and where other issues of local importance were discussed and organised. Nottinghamshire was divided into eight wapentakes by 1086 (fig. 14), but two of the smaller wapentakes were absorbed by others quite soon after this date. The six surviving wapentakes are Bassetlaw, Bingham, Broxtowe, Newark, Rushcliffe, and Thurgarton. Each wapentake had a main meeting place where people would assemble to undertake this kind of business, and probably also to trade, socialise, and play games and sports. Meeting places were multi-functional, and often made up of a number of smaller sites or features.

In some cases we know where the medieval assembly place of a wapentake was; occasionally there is documentary evidence which describes its function, but sometimes its name gives us this information instead. For example, Moothouse Pit was the meeting place for Bingham Wapentake, its name containing the Old English word *mot*, referring to a meeting or assembly of people. However, the evidence of a place-name alone doesn't tell us exactly when a place was used for this purpose, or by whom. We can sometimes infer this information from associated linguistic or archaeological evidence, but as the sites could be used for such a long period of time and for so many different purposes, the picture is often quite complicated.

Figure 14: Map of Nottinghamshire and its wapentakes
as described in the Domesday Book (1086).

Figure 15: Two Viking period re-enactors standing on top of the mound at Thynghowe. The Birklands Forest Stone can be seen to the right.

An intriguing site in Nottinghamshire is Thynghowe, situated near Hangar Hill in the Birklands area of Sherwood Forest. The place-name means 'assembly hill', from the Old Norse words *thing* and *haugr*. *Thing* was the word commonly used in Scandinavia for a place with this kind of function, and the modern Icelandic parliament, which has its roots in an assembly established in 930, is called the *Althingi*, derived from the same term. The place-name, then, points firmly to an administrative function for Thynghowe, and there is no reason to doubt the appropriateness of the name. Thynghowe is certainly a hill, perhaps even a man-made mound, and although it is difficult to see clearly when the surrounding undergrowth is flourishing, clearance of the mound has previously made it possible to see its full extent (fig. 15). Standing on top of such a hill would be an ideal place to address a large audience, which would have been a key function of a meeting-place. Until recently, however, no in-depth investigation of the site had been undertaken by archaeologists.

The Friends of Thynghowe have been working for years to have the site recognised for its historical significance, and in 2008 it was listed by English Heritage (now Heritage England) as a possible assembly place, although its origins remained unclear. Several surveys of the site were undertaken by different groups, and in 2013 an excavation of earthworks near Thynghowe revealed a large circular enclosure that likely dates to the early medieval period or perhaps even earlier (fig. 16). Unfortunately the archaeological finds from within the enclosure do not provide any conclusive evidence for either its date or its function, but it is possible that the earthworks are connected with the mound as part of a larger, multi-functional area, as is the case with many other

© Lynda Mallett, 2017, reproduced by kind permission. With thanks to the Friends of Thynghowe

Figure 16: Excavations of the earthworks at Thynghowe.

medieval assembly sites. The enclosure was cut into the side of the mound, showing that it must be of a later date than the mound itself. In 2015 and 2016, further geophysical surveys were undertaken, and these confirm the multi-functional nature of the site. These activities have revealed evidence of two possible hearths, a series of holloways (sunken trackways), a spread or mound of pot-boiler stones used to move heat from a fire to a cooking vessel, part of a parish boundary ditch, and several boundary stones including one known as the Birklands Forest Stone.

Although it cannot yet be proven that Thynghowe was used as an assembly site in the **Viking Age**, several different factors are consistent with it having this function at some stage, or stages, in its history. It appears to be a multi-functional site which has a mound suitable for assembly and an enclosure used for a different purpose; it is close to multiple parish boundaries, which is a common feature of assembly sites; and perhaps most importantly, its name not only labels it as an assembly place, but also suggests either that it was used by Viking settlers in the area, or that they knew of its use as such by the **Anglo-Saxons** prior to their arrival.

A group of place-names in the East Midlands may also have a role to play in understanding administration in the period following Viking settlement in the Danelaw: that is, the places called Normanton which cluster in the region. Nottinghamshire has five of these, two being simply Normanton (one near Southwell, one near Elkesley), and the other three being differentiated as Normanton on Trent, Normanton on Soar (both named from the nearby rivers), and Normanton on the Wolds. These names come from the Old English *Northmenn* – 'northmen, Vikings', and *tūn* – 'farm, village'. Although their names are in Old English, they indicate something Scandinavian about the settlements and their inhabitants, or perhaps the area in which the settlements are found, and the frequent recurrence of the name might mean that it was understood as a special kind of label. In the context of the Danelaw, and especially the English re-conquest in the early tenth century, it is possible that the significance of these names is administrative, marking places with a particular function in a region of notable Scandinavian settlement.

4. Viking Nottingham

The **Anglo-Saxon Chronicle** informs us that when King Edward 'the Elder' retook Nottingham from the Vikings in 918, he strengthened its defences, manning the garrison with both English and Danish men. This tells us a number of important things. First, that Nottingham had defences before this time, which were strengthened and built up during the **Viking Age**. Second, that Nottingham was important enough to invest in defending; not only did Edward strengthen existing defences, but he built a second *burh* on the opposite side of the river, giving him control of the Trent and of its crossings. Third, that Viking settlers or their descendants were not expelled from the city on its recapture, but accepted as its inhabitants, even trusted to defend it; we can assume that settlers would have remained in the rest of the county too.

The Viking history of the city of Nottingham is dealt with as a separate chapter here as the picture is slightly different. As we know from the documentary sources, the *burh* was conquered twice by the **Great Heathen Army** before it was re-taken by the English, and this means we have a more concrete picture of the military and political effect of the Viking Age in the city than we do in the rest of the county. We have more in the way of documentary evidence, though there is still very little evidence about the city in general. Because so much of Nottingham and its immediate surroundings are now urban, archaeological investigation is severely hampered and metal detector finds like those from rural areas cannot help us fill in the blanks. As already mentioned, the site of the Great Heathen Army's winter camp in or around Nottingham cannot be located for this exact reason, but there are some tools we can use to fill in some details about the later town. This section will detail the limited evidence we have for what Viking Nottingham might have looked like.

Figure 17: Map of the locations of the Drury Hill, Halifax Place and Woolpack Lane excavations in Nottingham.

Map data © 2017 Google. Map by the author

Figure 18: The excavations at Drury Hill, on the edge of Nottingham's medieval defences. The photograph shows a section across the early medieval ditch.

Digging the city

Between 1969 and 1980, excavations were undertaken at six sites in Nottingham to learn more about the medieval *burh* and the stages of the city's development (fig. 17). Several of these sites revealed important information about the **Anglo-Saxon** and Viking town and its defences. The early medieval settlement at Nottingham was in the part of the modern city roughly equivalent to the Lace Market, and the *burh's* defences surrounded this area. The current Nottingham Castle is a much later development – the first castle on that site was built after the Norman Conquest.

Excavations at Drury Hill, which took place between 1969 and 1970, revealed a defensive rampart and massive ditch outside it (fig. 18). The ditch cut through the remains of an earlier building, and evidence shows that it was re-cut in the time either shortly before or during the Viking occupation of Nottingham. This same pattern was shown at Woolpack Lane, with defences being improved at the same time as Drury Hill. This was, as documentary evidence would suggest, a time

Figure 19: The excavations at Halifax Place, in the heart of the Anglo-Saxon *burh* of Nottingham. Archaeologist Gordon Young is shown triangulating the northern edge of the early medieval defensive ditch, which runs top-bottom in the photograph.

when military defence was very important. The rampart and boundary ditch represent the ninth and tenth century defences which would have played a huge part in the *burh*'s resistance against first the Vikings, and then the English forces who re-took Nottingham in the tenth century. We know from the documentary sources that fortifications were improved and a second *burh* was built following the English re-conquest, and there may be some association between the re-cutting of the ditch and this phase of military improvement.

At Halifax Place, a site within the boundary of the *burh*, an earlier ditch was discovered (fig. 19), dated to between 650 and 850, and therefore predating the Viking presence in Nottinghamshire. Also found at this site were the remains of three different phases of large timber buildings, all used before the year 1000, which clearly demonstrates use of this site within both Anglo-Saxon and Viking Nottingham.

Viking town planning

The defences excavated at Woolpack Lane and Drury Hill form a boundary around the early medieval *burh*. Within this area a street plan developed, and the outline of the *burh* is still visible in the shape of the street plan today. If we use a suitable map in combination with the city's street-names, we can build up a strong picture of how the early medieval town took shape.

John Speed, a well-known historian and cartographer, drew a detailed map of Nottingham in 1610, complete with a key of all the street-names in use at that date (fig. 20). His map post-dates the Norman Conquest and the expansion of the city over a much larger area than early medieval Nottingham, but it is nevertheless the closest we have to a depiction of the early medieval *burh*. In some cases, the street-names Speed uses are recognisable in modern names, but some of them have been replaced since then, so it is important to have this early record. Halifax Place, where some of the archaeological excavations took place, can be located as *Hallifax Lane* on Speed's map. Drury Hill, however, used to be *Vault Lane*, as shown in 1610. The outline of the *burh* can be seen on Speed's map, with the boundary roughly level with Woolpack Lane and Warser Gate from east to west, then turning in a southerly direction to form the edges of a rectangle with rounded corners. You can see the correlation between the boundary ditch and the street layout within, explaining the street layout which would otherwise look quite muddled and random in this seventeenth-century depiction.

Even without the benefit of archaeological excavations, some of the street-names would certainly give us a clue as to the location of the ancient defences. Warser Gate (fig. 21), the road which follows the northern boundary of the *burh*, was first recorded as *The Wallsete* in 1331, deriving from the **Old English** words *weall* and *setu* and meaning 'buildings by the

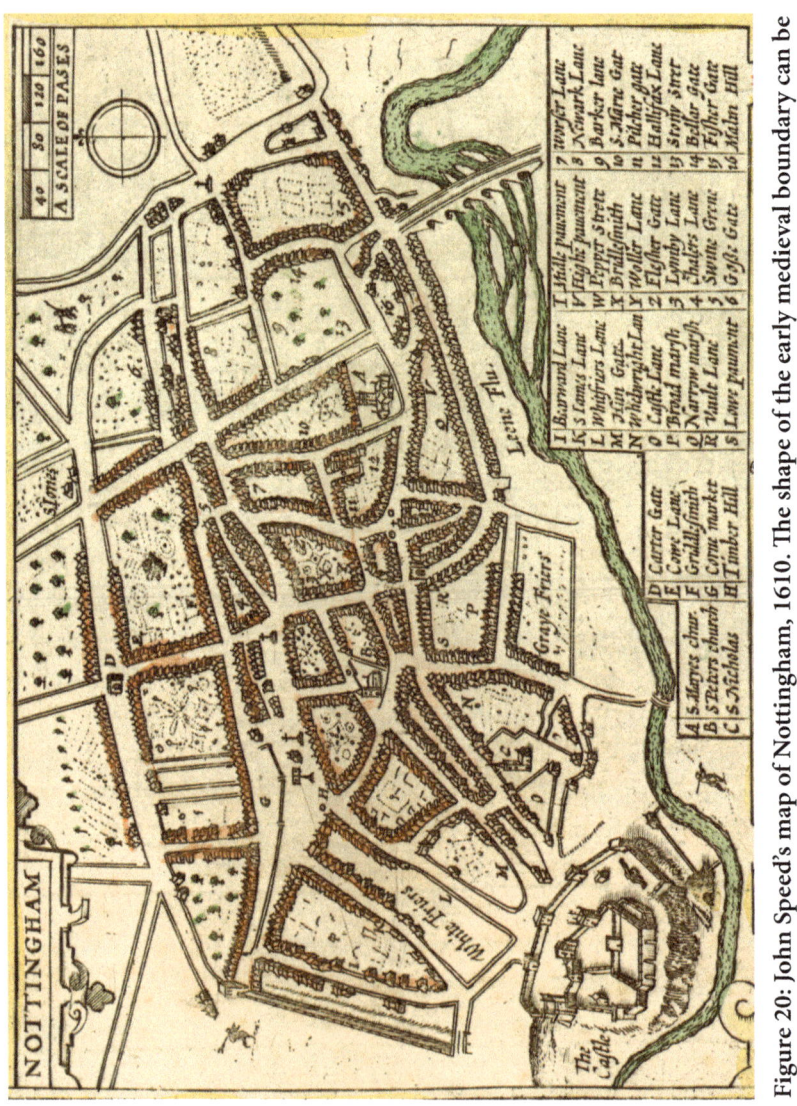

Figure 20: John Speed's map of Nottingham, 1610. The shape of the early medieval boundary can be seen in the layout of the streets in the east of the city. This map is held by the Manuscripts and Special Collections Department at the University of Nottingham, catalogue reference EMSC Not 1.B8.C76.

© University of Nottingham, 2017

wall'. The strip of land between the street and the rampart evidently contained houses, giving rise to the name of the street itself.

Other street-names don't necessarily tell us about the shape of the town, but they do tell their own story of Viking presence in the

Figure 21: The modern street sign on Warser Gate.

city, both within the medieval period and after it. If you know Nottingham, you'll know that many of its streets have names ending in -*gate*. This comes from the **Old Norse** word *gata*, referring to a road or a path. Not all of Nottingham's streets date back to the Viking Age, of course, but the terminology the Vikings used to refer to the early medieval town seems to have well and truly stuck. One example of a modern *gate* in medieval Nottingham is Fletcher Gate (fig. 22). It is first recorded in 1335 as *flesshewergate*, meaning 'street of the butchers' (flesh-hewers). On Speed's map the name is recorded as *Flesher Gate*, showing a half-way

point between the early spelling and the modern name. War-ser Gate, as we've seen, runs parallel to the early medieval defences, and though it isn't first recorded as a *gate*, it had certainly become one by 1435, when it is called *Wal-sedgate*.

Figure 22: The modern street sign on Fletcher Gate.

There are twenty-six street-names in the city of Nottingham which contain the word *gate*, some of which would have been named long after the Viking Age had ended. They begin to show that the language and layout of the city continued to be influenced by its Scandinavian settlers for many years to come, and that – just like York and Lincoln, two other places heavily influenced by Viking settlement – *gate*s became a permanent part of the city's character.

There are even some modern street-names which used to be *gate*s but have since been changed: evidence of Scandinavian influence hiding behind restructuring and renaming. Hollow Stone was *Hologate* in 1357, so called because it made its way through a steep rock connected with the town wall. Chapel Bar was once *Barregate* (1242), Friar Lane used to be *Motehallegate* (1329), referring to the old Moot Hall in Wheelergate; Mount Street, climbing towards the castle, was *Bereworde Gate* (1240), named from a bear 'ward' or keeper, presumably connected with the cruel sport of bear-baiting; Pelham Street was *Greytsmithisgate* in 1309, referring to smiths who had their workshops along it. Even main thoroughfares could be renamed: Derby Road was *Derbigate* in 1301, the modern name having exactly the same meaning but exchanging the Old Norse word for the English one.

Nottingham is not alone in having a cluster of *gate*s. Newark has its fair share, as do Southwell, Retford, Worksop and Mansfield: the influence of the Viking settlers on now-urban areas was not limited to Nottingham itself.

5. Integration

Nottingham's street-names already begin to show that Viking influence lasted far beyond the short time when Scandinavian settlers might have lived in separate communities and spoken a separate language from the **Anglo-Saxons**. The story of the Vikings in Nottinghamshire is ultimately one of integration and of the development of a shared culture and identity which is often termed **Anglo-Scandinavian**. This shared culture can be seen in a number of different types of evidence, created both immediately after the Viking settlement and in the centuries that followed.

The picture is complicated somewhat by the fact that Viking leadership over England did not come to a permanent end with the English re-conquest of the Danelaw. In the early eleventh century, Sveinn 'Forkbeard', King of Denmark (sometimes spelt Sweyn in English), made repeated raids on England. In 1013 he launched a full-scale invasion and became King of England, although he held the kingdom for less than two months. Sveinn died in 1014, and his son Knútr (Cnut or Canute) was driven out of England by the returning English king, only to return in 1016 and conquer England for himself. Knútr and his family ruled England for the next twenty-six years.

This might seem like a very brief explanation of a very important series of events, but the simple reason for this is that the eleventh century Danish conquests did not have the same dramatic effect on Nottinghamshire as the settlement of the ninth and tenth centuries. They cemented the place of the Viking settlers and their descendants in England, and introduced a new set of higher-status Danish landowners. These changes came at a time when those people who formed the original phase of Viking settlers were already a part of Nottinghamshire, and therefore the eleventh-century conquests of Sveinn and Knútr are, in a Nottinghamshire context, part of this process of integration. There are signs of their effect on Anglo-Scandinavian culture, but they simply enhanced the developments which were already well underway.

Carving out a new identity

Those people of Viking descent who had made Nottinghamshire their new home had ties to two different cultures: to their ancestral homelands in Scandinavia, and to their adopted home in England. Settlers with enough money and power found ways to articulate this new, Anglo-Scandinavian identity through objects, and some of the best examples of these objects are pieces of stone sculpture which survive from the period following the Viking settlement.

Stone sculpture was both expensive and time-consuming to create. First, stone blocks had to be either quarried for that purpose, or reused from other buildings or monuments, in many cases travelling long distances before being sculpted. Sculptures were then designed and carved by master craftsmen with the skill to work stone, a long and laborious task. Stone sculpture was not, therefore, commissioned on a whim, and every aspect of it would have been carefully considered for the message it would send. If sculpture survives in a good condition, and can be decoded sufficiently clearly, it is full of information not only about the way its commissioners saw themselves but, just as importantly, about the way they wanted to be remembered.

There is a range of different sculptures in Nottinghamshire which show Viking influence. Experts on medieval sculpture can use the designs and imagery chosen and depicted on each piece of sculpture to work out the date range when it is likely to have been carved, the cultural influences it shows, and the messages contained within it. The more complete the sculpture, naturally, the more confidently this information can be ascertained.

There are a handful of stone grave covers found in Nottinghamshire which have clear Scandinavian traits. They belong to a group of monuments known as '**hogbacks**', which have a ridge running

© Graeme Thornhill, 2017, with thanks to Gill and John Bloor

Figure 23: The hogback monument at St Luke's church, Hickling

lengthways along the centre of the stone and are curved so that the highest point is in the middle – the metaphor is a straightforward one, with the stones having the same shape as a hog's back. This type of sculpture is usually found in the north of England and southern Scotland, in areas of Viking settlement. Hogbacks are not found in Scandinavia, so they represent a new kind of sculpture created in England by Viking settlers who had converted to Christianity. The earliest examples are probably from the tenth century, and they seem to have fallen out of fashion by the twelfth. The examples in Nottinghamshire are unusual in being found so far south, and show a conscious choice to use sculpture associated with Anglo-Scandinavian culture, rather than imitating either Scandinavian or Anglo-Saxon monuments.

The hogback found at St Luke's Church in Hickling (fig. 23) is almost completely intact, with a single break between two parts of the stone

Figure 24: The Hickling hogback from above, showing the cross carved on the upper surface.

© Graeme Thornhill, 2017, with thanks to Gill and John Bloor

having been repaired. It seems to have been found underneath the chancel of the church in the early nineteenth century, and has been kept inside the church since its discovery, which means that it hasn't suffered a great deal from exposure to the elements and the carvings on it are still clear to see. The hogback's design contains features from a number of different sculptural traditions, and is consequently difficult to categorise. The stone out of which the hogback was carved probably comes from a Roman monument, perhaps in Leicester. Although the shape of this hogback is broader, longer and flatter than many others, this might be a consequence of the original shape of the stone rather than the choice of the sculptor. At the head and foot of the sculpture are two carved bears, a feature which is associated with classic hogback forms from the north of England. By contrast, however, on the top of the hogback is a cross, dividing the decoration (fig. 24); crosses are rarely found on hogbacks, and combining the bear motif with a cross can be seen as a way of mixing **heathen** Scandinavian traditions with Christian ones.

There are two ways of interpreting this sculpture. Either it is part of an early tenth-century group of monuments which are part of a Hiberno-Norse (Irish Viking) tradition associated with the Kingdom of York, or perhaps it is an early eleventh-century piece associated with new

Danish land ownership following Knútr's conquest of England. The latest research on the Hickling hogback puts it in that first group of sculptures, showing the influence of York in Nottinghamshire in the tenth century. In this context, the mixture of traditional Scandinavian motifs and new Christian symbolism can be seen as part of a phase of growing integration between Viking settlers and the English population, even in the case of Vikings wealthy and influential enough to commission stone sculpture.

Parts of two different hogbacks can now be found at St Mary and All Saints Church in Shelton. Like the Hickling stone, both were found under or near the chancel wall, and have been kept inside the church since

© Graeme Thornhill, 2017, with thanks to Rev. Liz Murray and to Marianne Howarth

Figure 25: One of the two hogbacks at Shelton, dated to around 950. This hogback is part of the 'Trent Valley' group.

the late nineteenth century. One of these stones dates to about 950, and the other is slightly later, likely from the last quarter of the tenth century. Both of them had been cut in half to be reused as building stones, and the remaining sections of the sculptures have not been found.

The earlier stone (fig. 25) is part of a distinctive East Midlands category of hogbacks termed the 'Trent Valley' group. Its carved interlace is simply a pattern, and does not contain any of the animal motifs that the Hickling stone shows. Like the Hickling monument, a cross shape was shown on the lid, and its ends characterise it as a 'wheel rim' type in which the head and foot have a semicircular profile. The second stone (fig. 26) is more elaborate than the first, and belongs to a type of hogback known as the 'warrior's tomb' shape, which would have looked more like a house. Dating from slightly later, this stone seems to represent a trans-

Figure 26: The second Shelton hogback, dated to the late tenth century. This is a transitional monument between the 'Trent Valley' and 'mid-Kesteven' types.

ition between the Trent Valley hogbacks, like the earlier Shelton stone, and a later group of sculpture called the 'mid-Kesteven' type, which is a simplification of the Trent Valley style. It does not fit comfortably into either category, but does demonstrate the progression of sculptural tradition in Nottinghamshire. Like the Hickling stone, these monuments portray traditional Scandinavian elements alongside newer

© Graeme Thornhill, 2017, with thanks to Sir Edward Nall and to Rev. Phil White

Figure 27: The Hoveringham tympanum, in its position reset above the main door at St Michael's church.

Christian iconography, creating affiliations with both cultures. Experts have seen these hogbacks as an indication of powerful individuals of Viking heritage demonstrating their affiliation with the English rulers following the early tenth century re-conquest of **Mercia**.

Viking influence on stone sculpture even continued after another change of leadership, the Norman Conquest of 1066. This is a turning-point in English history at which you might expect a severance from previous cultural traditions, but the process was not by any means as simple and clear-cut as this. The stone over the main door at St Michael's church in Hoveringham, known as the Hoveringham **tympanum** (fig. 27), is an example of Scandinavian influence continuing after 1066. The stone is in a version of the Urnes style – often termed the last phase of Viking art, it was used in Scandinavia from the mid-eleventh century to about 1150. It is characterised by slim and stylised animals with large, almond-shaped eyes, curly appendages on their noses and necks, and tightly interwoven patterns. There is an English variant of this art style, which is found both within and outside the **Danelaw**. It is thought,

© Graeme Thornhill, 2017, with thanks to Sir Edward Nall and to Rev. Phil White

Figure 28: Detail of the Urnes-style dragon on the lower panel of the Hoveringham tympanum, with its nose lappet and looped body.

however, to be more prevalent in areas where Scandinavian influence was seen as more 'acceptable'. In general the English style is less stylised, and its looping patterns are less complex. This Urnes variant developed from a Scandinavian source in an English context, just as the hogback monuments did.

The main panel of the Hoveringham tympanum depicts St Michael in combat with two dragons. St Michael was an especially popular saint among newly-converted Scandinavians, and his presence on the tympanum perhaps gives it an additional Viking leaning. Despite the obvious crack, the sculpture is made up of a single stone, divided into several panels. The lower, rectangular lintel panel shows two dragons and a semi-human winged creature, with St Peter on the far right and a priestly figure on the far left. The dragons on this stone are certainly in an Urnes style, and it has been argued that they share more similarities with Scandinavian Urnes dragons than English ones: their bodies are shown in complex double loops, and one of the dragons on the lower panel has a lappet (decorative flourish) on its head (fig. 28), a common feature of dragons in the Scandinavian Urnes style. Researchers believe that the tympanum has a strong association with the more famous Southwell lintel, located in Southwell Minster, and that it may have been part of the minster before it was restructured in the twelfth century.

Brooches, rings, and shiny things

Stone sculpture is not the only kind of artefact which demonstrates this new, Anglo-Scandinavian cultural identity. Jewellery, for example, could be used as an expression of cultural affiliation. Women's brooches had a function in Viking and Anglo-Saxon women's clothing, as they fastened dresses or cloaks, but they were worn in different ways in the different countries, and the fashions in brooches can be traced to different places and time periods. The pin fittings on the reverse of Anglo-Saxon brooches were different from Viking ones, and while Anglo-Saxon brooches were typically a flat disc shape, Scandinavian brooches came in many more shapes and styles. Anglo-Scandinavian brooches, made in England in the years following Viking settlement, could have a mix of both Anglo-Saxon and Scandinavian features, creating new types of brooch found only in the Danelaw.

The disc-shaped brooch in the photograph (fig. 29) dates from the tenth century and is probably Anglo-Scandinavian. It is made of a lead alloy, and might be designed to look like a gold coin. The bird-shaped brooch (fig. 30) is made of a copper alloy, and dates from sometime between 850 and 1000. It may be intended to resemble a cockerel, as the bird has a small crest on its head. This style is Scandinavian, but the

Figure 29: Lead alloy cast disc or plate brooch, found in north Nottinghamshire and dated to the tenth century. Information is available on the Portable Antiquities Scheme database, under find number NLM-879595.

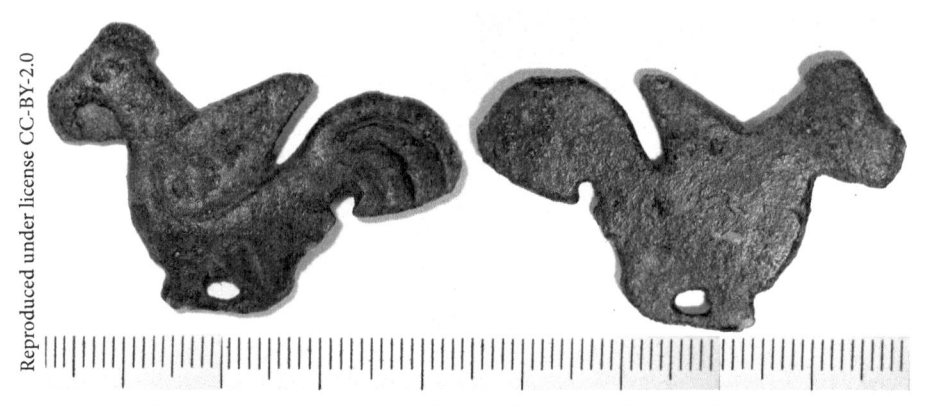

Figure 30: Cast copper alloy brooch (unfinished) in the shape of a bird, possibly a cockerel. Dated between 850 and 1000, and found in eastern Nottinghamshire. Information is available on the Portable Antiquities Scheme database, under find number DENO-0604D2.

distinctive curved shape of the bird's tail isn't usually found on Scandinavian brooches. These brooches are examples of the kind of jewellery women would have worn in Nottinghamshire in the Anglo-Scandinavian period, whether their ancestors were Anglo-Saxon or Scandinavian. Different brooch styles could be deliberately chosen to emphasise a woman's own heritage, or to intentionally adopt aspects of another culture, either to express association with a new family, to integrate with a culture she wanted to feel part of, or simply to follow fashion. Although these two Nottinghamshire examples were not found in the context of burials, brooches are frequently found as **grave goods** in the **Viking Age**. Just as weapons can be seen as a symbol of masculinity, brooches can be seen as one of femininity, and can carry messages about cultural, familial and societal roles and affiliations in death just as they could in life.

Another type of artefact which can be seen as Anglo-Scandinavian is a 'stirrup-strap mount' – a decorative piece of metal which was attached to stirrup leathers and connected them with stirrups themselves. Evidence suggests that metal stirrups were not widely used in England before the Viking Age, and that Danish settlers brought with them this kind of equestrian equipment. Two examples from Nottinghamshire are shown, both made of a copper alloy (figs. 31 & 32). They are different shapes and designs, but both date to the

Figures 31 & 32: Copper alloy Anglo-Scandinavian stirrup-strap mounts, dated to the eleventh century. Information is available on the Portable Antiquities Scheme database, under find numbers NLM-09E2D1 and DENO-6F42D6.

eleventh century, apparently giving them an Anglo-Scandinavian origin.

There are other artefacts which cannot necessarily be attributed to an Anglo-Scandinavian culture, but which point to people of Scandinavian origin, or with Viking connections, going about their daily business in Nottinghamshire. Coins had long been in use as currency in England, but in the Danelaw they occurred alongside **bullion** used as payment. A bullion economy was present in Scandinavia and other areas in the north and east of Europe; in other words, this is the currency that Vikings brought with them. To be of any use, silver bullion had to be weighed to determine its value. Therefore, pieces of silver of various sizes, and weights and scales used to measure them by traders, are both indicators of this 'dual-currency' economy which was certainly functioning into the tenth century in the

Figure 33: Silver bullion found near Newark in 1995, dated to between 870 and 950. Information is available on the Portable Antiquities Scheme database, under find number NLM-1B0476.

Danelaw. These kinds of items were also found by archaeologists on the site of the **Great Heathen Army**'s winter camp at Torksey.

The silver used in a bullion economy could come in many forms, from adapted items such as cut silver coins and jewellery, to specially-made ingots. Such a group of silver pieces, at least one of which is an ingot, was found close to Newark in 1995 (fig. 33). It was discovered close to a piece of a gold finger ring which is also thought to have been used as bullion. Some of the silver pieces seem to correspond to the weight units used either in Scandinavia or in Viking Dublin, so there is a strong probability that the silver would have been used for trade in Anglo-Scandinavian Nottinghamshire, perhaps in nearby Newark. An example of a lead weight which would have been used to measure such silver bullion was found in north Nottinghamshire in 2011 (fig. 34). As with the silver, this weight seems to correspond to the system of units used in Scandinavian-derived measuring systems. Together, this kind of evidence points to a Scandinavian economic system functioning in this part of England in the ninth or tenth centuries. Added to the picture of the Great Heathen Army that has emerged from the excavations at Torksey, this can be taken as further

Figure 34: Lead weight found in north Nottinghamshire in 2011, dated to between 900 and 1050. The discoloured patch on the top of the weight looks like something may have been embedded in it, perhaps a coin. Information is available on the Portable Antiquities Scheme database, under find number NLM-941282.

demonstration that Viking settlers were craftsmen and traders, and not only warriors and conquerors.

Sharing space: mixed-language place-names

It's not only places that are named entirely in the **Old Norse** language which show us where Viking settlers may have lived. There are also place-names made up of two or more words, combining **Old English** and Old Norse. We can't always know whether the people who named the places were speakers of Norse or English, but the fact that words from both languages were being used in these names means that the two different communities were communicating with each other enough to borrow each other's words, at the very least, and they may even have been living in the same settlements, although this is hard to prove.

An interesting type of name is the combination of Old Norse given names, usually (but not always) men's names, with the Old English word *tūn* – 'farm, village'. For example, Gonalston in Nottinghamshire means 'Gunnulf's farm or village', while Thoroton belonged to Thurferth. Different theories have been presented as to what this pattern of names means, but it seems likely that the given names represent landowners, either Vikings who had been granted land immediately after the initial phase of conquest, or people who came to own that land in the decades which followed it. It's possible that the names are replacements of, or changes to, existing Old English names, but it's also possible that the Viking settlers borrowed the English word *tūn* and used it in brand new names. The equivalent Old Norse word, *tún*, is sometimes used in Scandinavia, although not so frequently as in England.

Other names seem simply to have been made up of words from the two different languages. Eastwood, for example, actually comes from the Old English word *east* and the Old Norse word *thveit* – 'clearing' (sometimes place-names aren't as straightforward as they seem!), while Maplebeck is from Old English *mapol* – 'maple tree', and Old Norse

© the author and Graeme Thornhill, 2017

Figure 35: Map of mixed-language parish names in
Nottinghamshire, shown alongside the entirely Old Norse
parish names depicted on the map in fig. 6 (p. 24).

bekkr – 'stream'. There are thirty-two mixed-language parish names in Nottinghamshire, which are marked on the map alongside the entirely Old Norse names (fig. 35).

The influence of the Old Norse language isn't only found through its words being used, but also in the way some Old English words are pronounced. As anybody who has tried to learn another language will know, particular sounds can be very difficult to pronounce correctly if they are unfamiliar, and don't occur in your own language. Viking settlers had particular trouble with soft (voiceless palatal) sounds like 'sh' [ʃ] and 'ch' [tʃ], and many place-names in Nottinghamshire seem to have been pronounced differently to help the Old Norse speakers cope with this problem! Usually when names were written down in the medieval and early modern periods, the spelling reflected the way they were pronounced, which is very helpful for place-name experts. Fiskerton near Southwell should have been *Fisherton* according to Old English pronunciation, but instead changed from 'sh' [ʃ] to 'sk' [sk] under Viking influence. This same sound change can be found elsewhere in Nottinghamshire too, for example in Askham (fig. 36).

Sometimes we can't be sure whether Old English or Old Norse words were originally used in place-names, as they were so similar: the Old English word for 'church' was *cirice*, pronounced with a 'ch' [tʃ], while the Old Norse word was *kirkja*, with a hard 'k' [k]. Words in different languages which derive from the same root in this way are called **cognates**, and they can be difficult to tell apart in situations of close language contact such as Anglo-Scandinavian England. Place-names containing 'kirk' such as Kirklington are certainly pronounced in the Old Norse way, but some of them may have originally been Old English names. The Kirkbys, however, are formed with Old Norse *bý*, and are therefore likely to be entirely Old Norse names. The many Carltons in Nottinghamshire were formed with either Old English *ceorl* or the cognate Old Norse *karl*, both meaning 'peasant'. Again, the Old English word was pronounced with a soft 'ch' [tʃ] rather than a hard 'k' [k], but the form and pronunciation which survives today is the Scandinavian

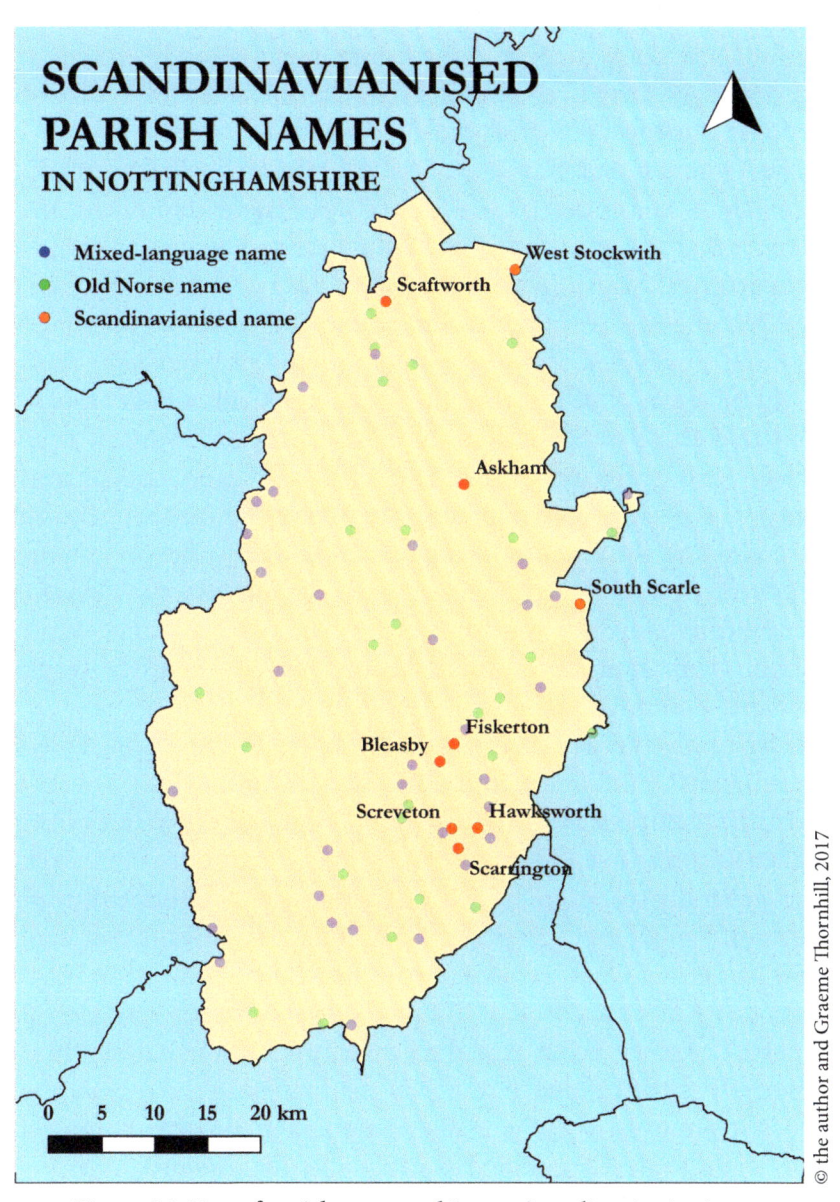

Figure 36: Map of parish names subject to Scandinavianisation, shown alongside entirely Old Norse and mixed-language parish names depicted on the previous place-name maps.

one. The Carltons in Nottinghamshire mean exactly the same as Charltons elsewhere in the country, but the rule of thumb is that where you find Charltons, you don't find Vikings.

Place-name researchers can't always determine what form a name originally took, as often by the time it was first written down, Viking influence had affected the pronunciation so much that it looks like Old Norse even if it wasn't. In some rare cases, we know that part of an Old English name was replaced by Old Norse: the village of Bleasby, near Southwell, was *Blisetune* in 958, with the Old English *tūn* being replaced by Old Norse *bý*, both having the meaning 'farm, village'. Does this mean that the Viking settlers understood the meaning of the Old English word, and used it interchangeably with an equivalent word in their own language? Unfortunately we'll never be sure, but Bleasby is an interesting and unusual example. The same process certainly happened elsewhere, but it is rare to have documentary evidence of it. The Nottinghamshire parish names subject to some kind of Scandinavianisation are shown on the map (fig. 36) alongside the purely Old Norse and mixed-language place-names discussed above.

It isn't only the names of towns and villages which preserve Old Norse linguistic influence: it can also be seen in the names of smaller landscape features in Nottinghamshire. However, the names of these smaller features (usually called **minor names** by place-name experts) aren't generally recorded in early documents; it's unusual to find them written down before the late twelfth century. That means that we can't know for certain whether they were in use during the Viking Age, and it's probably more accurate to think about Old Norse words in minor names as a post-Viking Age dialect feature. Nevertheless, this still demonstrates the influence of Viking settlement in the region, even if it doesn't show exactly where Viking settlers made their homes. If we think about settlers speaking two languages in close proximity to one another, the speakers of Old English probably borrowed vocabulary from Old Norse where it was useful and appropriate for them, and when people of Viking descent began speaking Old English, it makes sense for them to have continued using some words from Old Norse as part of this process. Some of those Old Norse words were thoroughly absorbed into the language of the local Anglo-Scandinavian people, and became part of a Norse-influenced Nottinghamshire dialect.

Many of Nottinghamshire's streams are called *becks*, from the Old Norse word *bekkr*. This same word has been adopted into modern English dialect across much of northern England. You might also be familiar with *dykes*, which derive either from Old Norse *dík* or the cognate Old English *dīc*, but which have a Scandinavianised pronunciation in Nottinghamshire, with a hard 'k' [k] instead of a soft 'ch' [tʃ]. In non-Scandinavianised parts of the country, this word generally becomes *ditch*. These are some of the names you're more likely to notice in the modern landscape, but there are other Norse words you might spot that are retained in the names of fields, and which sometimes survive in street names in rural parts of the county, where those streets have been constructed next to or on top of the field which originally bore the name. You might see a *wong*, from Old Norse *vangr*, a word for a particular type of enclosure: in Southwell, for example, there is a small residential street called Lowes Wong, and an infant school with the same name. Other common Nottinghamshire words to look out for are *howe*, from Old Norse *haugr* 'mound, hill'; *holme*, from *holmr* 'wet meadow'; *dale*, usually from Old Norse *dalr* 'valley'; and *lyng* 'heather, gorse'.

Place-names are one of the clearest ways to see Viking influence on local language, and they can show everything from names given by the first Viking settlers to their farms and villages to names given by people in later centuries to features in their landscape using words they probably didn't even know were derived from Old Norse.

6. The end of Viking Nottinghamshire?

This book has covered just a small selection of the evidence for Viking Nottinghamshire, and even from a potted history it's clear what an enormous contribution Viking settlement has made to the unique character of this county, from its place-name dialect to its administrative units and the terminology which describes them. That contribution can be seen in those things we all think of as historical artefacts: archaeological evidence, from metal detector finds to professional digs; documentary evidence in medieval manuscripts; and even the style and imagery found on stone sculpture. But the kind of evidence people sometimes forget is the evidence we can see in the present, which you don't have to look at in photographs, or view in a museum or archive. There are parts of Viking Nottinghamshire which remain in the present day, for anyone who knows where to look. You can walk the streets of Anglo-Scandinavian Nottingham, and follow Warser Gate along the line of the medieval town wall. You can look at signposts as you pass, and notice common Old Norse words in place-names, and you can see a reflection of the wapentakes that made up Viking Nottinghamshire in the names of some of our modern administrative districts. And now that you're armed with the knowledge of where to find them, you can see not only these modern reflections of the Viking Age, but you can go to see the stone sculptures photographed in this book, artefacts of Anglo-Scandinavian Nottinghamshire which can still, in some cases, be found in the places they would have resided in the medieval period.

If you're interested in learning more about the topics this book has touched upon, I'd encourage you to look at the further information section at the back of the book. It gives suggestions for starting points, whether you want book recommendations, web resources, or places to go to see artefacts first-hand. Wherever you go from here, you'll go there in the knowledge that the Viking Age didn't end when the people of English and Scandinavian descent developed a shared culture rather than perpetuating their differences, or even when the Norman aristocrats imposed a new leadership on England in the eleventh century. Viking Nottinghamshire endures to this day, and all you have to do is get out there and see it.

Glossary

Anglo-Saxon
A term used to describe the people who settled in south-eastern Britain from the fifth century onwards. Bede, a monk and historian writing in the late seventh century, tells us that they were made up of three tribes: Angles, Saxons, and Jutes. The real picture is likely to have been far more complicated than this, but the general idea that the Anglo-Saxons began as a number of different groups of settlers is certainly correct. These groups eventually joined together to form kingdoms, although there were still local and regional groupings within those kingdoms. The Anglo-Saxons spoke a language called **Old English**.

Anglo-Saxon Chronicle
A set of manuscripts which document the important events which took place each year in **Anglo-Saxon** England. The Chronicle was created late in the ninth century, and began by recording historic events. Multiple copies were made of this original manuscript, and they were all updated independently by monks from different monasteries across England. Nine different manuscripts survive in some form (seven held in the British Library and one each in the Bodleian Library, Oxford, and the Parker Library of Corpus Christi College, Cambridge), and they each contain different details according to their own focus and bias. The Chronicle is one of the few documentary sources for events in early Anglo-Saxon and **Viking Age** England.

Anglo-Scandinavian
The culture which emerged in England following Viking settlement. The phrase can describe people, places, styles of clothing, jewellery or art, and even language or dialect. Objects which are interpreted as being Anglo-Scandinavian often combine features from both **Anglo-Saxon** and Scandinavian styles, and have developed additional traits unique to their context in Anglo-Scandinavian England.

bullion

Precious metal used as currency. Bullion could either consist of specially-made ingots, or of things like coins and jewellery broken or cut into pieces and valued by weight. The Scandinavian economy in the **Viking Age** used bullion rather than coins.

burh

A fortified settlement. These would often be found in locations which controlled key routeways or resources, and many were built during the **Viking Age**.

cognate

Cognates are words in different languages which derive from the same root. For example, the words for 'star' in many European languages are cognates, as they all developed from the same word in an ancient language called Indo-European. Some of these are recognisable as being related to the English word (for example Scots *starn*, Icelandic *stjarna*, Norwegian and Danish *stjerne* and German *Stern*), but some groups of languages have developed differently and the cognate words are less easy to spot (for example French *étoile*, Spanish *estrella*, Greek *asteri*, Armenian *astl*). **Old English** and **Old Norse** are very closely-related languages, from a language family known as Germanic, and their cognates would have been easy to spot for speakers of those languages, although sometimes they had slightly different meanings. For example, Old English *brycg* meant 'bridge', while the cognate Old Norse *bryggja* meant 'jetty' or 'landing place'.

Danelaw

The area controlled by Viking rulers in the late ninth century. Although it was largely retaken by English kings in the early tenth century, it was still perceived as separate from the rest of England for many years.

Domesday Book

A survey of England made in 1086 on the orders of William the Conqueror, the first **Norman** king of England. He wanted to record the amount of tax paid in previous years in order to assess wealth and power in his new kingdom. The survey was made in medieval Latin by Anglo-Norman scribes.

Five Boroughs

A confederation of five *burh*s, four of which would later become county towns: Derby, Leicester, Lincoln, Nottingham and Stamford.

grave goods

Possessions buried alongside a deceased person, usually in non-Christian (**heathen**) burials. These could be items signifying the deceased's role during their life, or could be items intended to accompany them in the afterlife.

Great Heathen Army

The name the **Anglo-Saxon Chronicle** gives to the Viking army which landed in East Anglia in 865 and conquered much of England by the end of the ninth century. Historians and archaeologists have spent many years trying to learn more about the army, how large it was, and who was a part of it.

heathen

Generally used to refer to someone who isn't part of a widely-held religion; in the context of Vikings it indicates a non-Christian. The Vikings who settled in England were not Christian when they arrived, in contrast to the Anglo-Saxons who had been converted to Christianity in the seventh century. In the **Anglo-Saxon Chronicle** in particular, the word is used to emphasise the cultural differences between the 'invading' Vikings and the 'native' **Anglo-Saxons**. The Viking religion in the early **Viking Age** was one of multiple gods, and most of what we know about them is from stories told in later centuries. You'll probably be familiar with the names of gods such as Thor and Odin, but it's important to remember that there were many other gods too, and that the introduction of a Christian god would likely not have been as shocking to the heathen Vikings as is sometimes thought. Christian imagery mixing with the older myths and legends probably wasn't an odd idea to the newly-converted Vikings in England.

hogback
A stone monument found in northern England in areas of significant Viking settlement. Hogbacks were used as grave markers, and their name comes from their shape, which is elongated with a central ridge, and slightly arched in the middle like a hog's back. This style of sculpture was created by Viking settlers who had converted to Christianity after settling in England.

hundred
An administrative unit of land made up of multiple parishes, smaller than a county.

Mercia
One of the main kingdoms of **Anglo-Saxon** England. Nottingham was within the kingdom of Mercia.

minor name
The name of a small landscape feature of local significance such as a field, hill, wood or stream.

Norman
The Normans were originally Viking settlers, who made their home in northern France and gave their name (northman, or Norseman) to the region of Normandy. Unlike the Vikings in England, they assimilated to the culture of France at that time and were therefore a culturally

different group from the **Anglo-Scandinavians**, despite their shared origins. After the death of the English King Edward the Confessor, who had no children, the claim to the English throne was disputed. Duke William II of Normandy was related to Edward, and fought at the Battle of Hastings in 1066 for the chance to become King of England. After his victory, he was known as William the Conqueror and the rest, as they say, is history.

Old English
The language spoken by the **Anglo-Saxons**. English has come under the influence of so many other languages since the early medieval period that modern English bears little resemblance to Old English.

Old Norse
The language spoken by the Vikings who settled in England. The Old Norse languages continued to be used for several centuries after the **Viking Age** in Scandinavia and Iceland, but when Old Norse is referred to in this book, it indicates the spoken language of the ninth and tenth century Viking settlers.

tympanum
A semi-circular decorative surface above a door, window or other entranceway, generally supported by a lintel and surrounded by an arch.

Viking Age
The period in which seafaring Scandinavians travelled, conquered and settled across much of western Europe and beyond. In this book the term 'Viking Age' is used to indicate the time period when Vikings were active in and around England, from the late eighth century until the **Normans** arrived in 1066.

wapentake

The term for a **hundred** used in the **Danelaw**, from an Old Norse compound word made up of *vápn* – 'weapon' and *taka* – 'to take'. It's not quite clear what the word indicated (suggestions have ranged from raising weapons as a means of voting to weapons being left outside the wapentake assembly site before entering), or whether it was even used literally in an English context.

Want more Vikings?

Online resources

A Church Near You
www.achurchnearyou.com
Many churches are unable to remain unlocked for visitors all the time, so if you want to go on a stone sculpture hunt, you'll need to check in advance that the sculpture is accessible. The Church of England website allows you to search for churches and find details on their opening hours and contact information for churchwardens. The stone sculptures featured in the book were accessed with the assistance of very helpful vicars and church-wardens, who were keen to have their sculpture admired!

The Corpus of Anglo-Saxon Stone Sculpture
www.ascorpus.ac.uk
This website contains information about the series of volumes of the *Corpus of Anglo-Saxon Stone Sculpture*, of which Nottinghamshire is number twelve. The first six volumes have been made available online, so you can view the full text and associated maps, drawings and photographs for County Durham and Northumberland; Cumberland, Westmorland and Lancashire-North-of-the-Sands; York and Eastern Yorkshire; South-East England; Lincolnshire; and Northern Yorkshire completely free on the website. Being the newest volume, the *Corpus* for Nottinghamshire has not been made available online, but see below for information about the book and where to access it.

The Key to English Place-Names
kepn.nottingham.ac.uk
The Key to English Place-Names is a free interactive tool from the Institute for Name-Studies at the University of Nottingham which allows you to look up place-names and discover their origins, meanings, and the languages they were named in. You can also investigate patterns

of place-names using the map interface. If you have an iPhone or iPad, there is also a free app available through the Apple store.

Portable Antiquities Scheme database
finds.org.uk
The website of the Portable Antiquities Scheme allows you to browse and search for artefacts and view photographs and information about them. Any of the artefacts discussed in this book can be found on the database using their find numbers, and you can explore similar items from within Nottinghamshire and elsewhere.

Centre for the Study of the Viking Age
www.nottingham.ac.uk/csva
The CSVA website contains information about everything that's happening in Viking Studies in Nottingham. There are frequent public events that you can attend, from lectures to exhibitions, and registration information is available online.

Friends of Thynghowe
www.thynghowe.org.uk
This website contains information about Thynghowe and its possible Viking Age context, as well as links to map, walking routes, leaflets, archaeological reports, and other online resources.

Recommended reading

This is just a small selection of the wide range of excellent books available on the Viking Age and the topics which are touched on in this book. Some are produced for a wide readership and are inexpensive to buy, while others are not. All are available in libraries across Nottinghamshire and elsewhere. All these books have extensive bibliographies you can use to follow up on any topics you'd like to learn more about.

The Viking Age

The Vikings in Britain and Ireland
by Jayne Carroll, Stephen H. Harrison and Gareth Williams (The British Museum, 2016)
A well-illustrated book on the impact of the Vikings in the whole of Britain and Ireland, drawing on the collections of the British Museum and written by experts in the field. Full of fascinating artefacts that you can view at the British Museum itself.

Vikings: Raids, Culture, Legacy
by Roderick Dale and Marjolein Stern (Andre Deutsch, 2016)
This is certainly the best-illustrated book about the Viking world to date, with photographs, drawings, pull-out replica manuscripts, maps and diagrams, and other memorabilia, as well as brilliant discussion of the Viking world from its origins to its legacy.

The Viking Diaspora
by Judith Jesch (Routledge, 2015)
The Viking Diaspora is all about Scandinavian settlement and migration, not only in Britain but elsewhere across northern Europe, illuminating the big picture of the Viking Age. If you're interested in a thorough discussion of shared culture and heritage that doesn't shy away from the complex topics, this book is definitely for you.

The Viking World
by James Graham-Campbell (Frances Lincoln, 2013)
This book discusses the Viking Age from a broad perspective, and contains chapters on religion, art, trade and industry, home life, writing and literature, ships and seafaring, exploration, warfare, and government. It's well-illustrated and uses a broad range of different types of evidence to build a picture of the Viking world.

The East Midlands in the Early Middle Ages
by Pauline Stafford (Leicester University Press, 1985)
For a fuller discussion of East Midlands history from the end of Roman Britain to the Norman Conquest, this is an excellent book. It's not as easy to get hold of in bookshops or online as some of the more recent books, but it's available through libraries.

Archaeology and artefacts

The Corpus of Anglo-Saxon Stone Sculpture, Volume XII: Nottinghamshire
by Paul Everson and David Stocker (Oxford University Press and the British Academy, 2016).
This is a large reference work which is expensive to buy, but well worth consulting. As well as being a catalogue of Nottinghamshire's Anglo-Saxon and Viking stone sculpture, it also contains extensive discussion sections exploring the significance of patterns in sculpture and the influences they show. If you find some sculpture you're interested in visiting, make sure you use the website 'A Church Near You' to check churches' opening hours.

50 Finds from Nottinghamshire and Derbyshire: Objects from the Portable Antiquities Scheme
by Alastair Willis (Amberley Publishing, 2016)
This book showcases archaeological finds recorded by the PAS scheme

in Nottinghamshire and Derbyshire, including full-colour illustrations and information about each artefact. It's written by the Finds Liaison Officer for the two counties, and is one of a set of books covering different parts of the country.

Place-names

A Dictionary of British Place-Names
by A.D. Mills (Oxford University Press, 2003)
A pocket-sized dictionary of all the major city, town and village names in Britain – everybody should have one. I take mine on car journeys and look up interesting names I see along the way (but not if I'm driving, obviously!).

The Place-Names of Nottinghamshire
by J.E.B. Gover, Allen Mawer and F.M. Stenton (English Place-Name Society, 1940)
This book covers the names not only of towns and villages, but also the names of much smaller places including hills, woods, waterways and even some fields. This is the only reliable book on Nottinghamshire place-names, and although it is expensive to buy online, it can be purchased directly either used or new from the English Place-Name Society at a lower price. See epns.org for more information.

Signposts to the Past
by Margaret Gelling (Phillimore, 2010)
Signposts explains the way place-names work and what they can tell us about the various stages of settlement and language use in Britain, including the Vikings and Old Norse. It's an excellent introduction to place-names as historical evidence.

Places to visit

Your local library
Libraries are an amazing (and free!) source of information, and they hold many of the books that are too expensive for most people to buy. Many libraries have specific local history sections, and librarians will be happy to help you find what you're looking for. You can find library information by visiting www.nottinghamcity.gov.uk/libraries if you live in the city, or www.nottinghamshire.gov.uk/culture-leisure/libraries for the rest of the county.

The Collection Museum, Lincoln (free admission)
This museum has a fascinating range of Viking and Anglo-Scandinavian artefacts which provide a vivid picture of life in Viking Age Lincoln.
www.thecollectionmuseum.com

Derby Museum and Art Gallery (free admission)
Derby Museum has an archaeology gallery full of local finds from the prehistoric to the eighteenth century.
www.derbymuseums.org/locations/museum-art-gallery

The British Museum, London (free admission)
This one is more out of the way, but if you're ever in London, do pay it a visit. The British Museum has extensive collections relating to the Viking Age (some of them discussed in *The Vikings in Britain and Ireland* – see above) and is open daily.
www.britishmuseum.org

Jorvik Viking Centre, York
Jorvik Viking Centre is built on the site where excavations in the 1970s and 1980s revealed the houses, workshops and back yards of the city of Jorvik as it stood in the Viking Age. Visits to the Centre include a journey through a reconstruction of Viking Age streets where you can

experience life as it would have been in tenth century York, including people speaking authentic Old Norse!
www.jorvikvikingcentre.co.uk

The Yorkshire Museum, York
The Yorkshire Museum has one of the most comprehensive archaeology collections in a regional British museum outside London. Most of their medieval objects come from York and Yorkshire (one of our neighbouring counties, don't forget!), including Anglo-Scandinavian material comparable to the artefacts discussed in this book.
www.yorkshiremuseum.org.uk

874

REPTON WINTER CAMP

The Great Heathen Army takes Repton, an important Mercian royal and ecclesiastical centre, and spends the winter there in 874/5.

878

CREATION OF THE DANELAW

A treaty is signed between King Alfred "the Great" of Wessex and Guthrum of the Danes, and an area of Danish rule in England is created.

865

GREAT HEATHEN ARMY LANDS IN ENGLAND

A group described as the "Great Heathen Army" by the Anglo-Saxon Chronicle lands in East Anglia and begins its journey across England. The army is made up of multiple groups of people under joint leadership, and consists of fighting men, craftspeople and traders, as well as women and children.

VIKING NOTTINGHAMSHIRE

793

LINDISFARNE RAID

Vikings raid the monastery of St Cuthbert on the island of Lindisfarne. The raid is recorded in the Anglo-Saxon Chronicle, and marks the beginning of the Viking Age in England.

873

TORKSEY WINTER CAMP

The Great Heathen Army spends the winter of 873/4 at Torksey in Lincolnshire, before moving west to Repton.

868

NOTTINGHAM WINTER CAMP

The Great Heathen army spends the winter of 868/9 in Nottingham.

1013

SVEINN BECOMES KING

The Danish King Sveinn becomes king of England, but dies only a few months later.

1066

THE NORMAN CONQUEST

William "the Conqueror" invades England from Normandy and takes the throne. This is the end of the Viking Age in England.

918

NOTTINGHAM RECAPTURED

King Edward "the Elder" recaptures Nottingham for the English, and begins improving its defenses..

KEY EVENTS

1016

KNÚTR BECOMES KING

Sveinn's son Knútr becomes king of England, and he and his family rule the country for the next 26 years.

Acknowledgements

This book was made possible by a grant from the University of Nottingham's British Identities Research Priority Area, and was written as part of the project 'Bringing Vikings Back to the East Midlands', in connection with the 'Danelaw Saga' exhibition, held at the Weston Gallery on University Park in the winter of 2017–18. I would like to thank all those who masterminded the project for giving me the opportunity to be involved, but especially Judith Jesch and Ross Bradshaw, without whom *Viking Nottinghamshire* could not have been produced.

Throughout the research and writing process, I have had assistance from many people, whether commenting on drafts, taking photographs, facilitating site visits, or simply answering questions and offering advice. I am grateful to all those people, and would like to thank John Baker, Gill and John Bloor, Stuart Brookes, Jayne Carroll, Roderick Dale, the Friends of Thynghowe, Rachel Gregory, Marianne Howarth, Cat Jarman, Lynda Mallett, Liz Murray, Edward Nail, Josh Neal, Malcolm Péadon, Ellie Rye, the Staffordshire Place-Name Study group, Graeme Thornhill, Phil White, and Alastair Willis for being so generous with their time and their wisdom, and Pippa Hennessy for making the book look as gorgeous as it does.